Contents

1. Early History 7
2. The Woodcut in America 29
3. A Modern Art Form 45
4. Projects and Demonstrations 71

TWENTIETH CENTURY WOODCUTS

TWENTIETH CENTURY WOODCUTS

History and Modern Techniques

Norman Laliberté   Alex Mogelon

An Art Horizons Book

Van Nostrand Reinhold Company
New York Cincinnati London Toronto Melbourne

To Jacques

Copyright © 1971 by Art Horizons, Inc.
Library of Congress Catalog Card No. 79-150507

Design consultant: Milton Glaser
Type set by Lettick Typografic, Inc.
Printed by Halliday Lithograph Corporation
Bound by Publishers Book Bindery

Published by Van Nostrand Reinhold Company
A Division of Litton Educational Publishing, Inc.
450 West 33rd Street, New York, N.Y. 10001
Published simultaneously in Canada by
Van Nostrand Reinhold Ltd.

16 15 14 13 12 11 10 9 8 7 6 5 4 3 2 1

Also by the authors:
The Art of Stencil (1971)
Collage, Montage, Assemblage (1971)
Drawing with Ink (1970)
Drawing with Pencils (1969)
Silhouettes, Shadows and Cutouts (1968)
Painting with Crayons (1967)
Banners and Hangings by Norman Laliberté
and Sterling McIlhany (1966)
Wooden Images by Norman Laliberté
and Maureen Jones (1966)

Frontispiece:
Fifteenth century wood
initial from Lyons,
France, printing center of
that time.

Opposite Page

Woodcut detail from *I
Giochi*, eighteenth
century Italian book of
games.

Egyptian hieroglyphics
carved in wood from the
Third Dynasty (third
millenium B.C.). Despite
the efforts of scholars
beginning in the sixth
century, hieroglyphics
remained a mystery until
1798 when an officer
serving Napoleon in his
conquest of Egypt
discovered the famous
Rosetta Stone, whose
multi-lingual inscriptions
made possible the
deciphering of the ancient,
stylized script.

1.
Early History

The history of the woodcut is a fascinating chapter in the evolution of man's ability to communicate through an art medium.

The woodcut originated in the Far East where, over two thousand years ago, carved or engraved wooden blocks were used to make symbolic, decorative, and religious design impressions on clay or wax surfaces.

By the second century A.D., the Chinese were wood block printing on paper, a technique which was soon to be introduced in Japan as a religious art form. Though the Phoenicians were known to have brought Indian wood block printed fabrics westward before the time of Alexander the Great, woodcut printing developed in Europe only as paper became readily available.

In the eleventh century, with the import of paper from the Far East, some woodcut printing took place in Spain. However, it was not until paper began to be manufactured in Germany and France at the turn of the fourteenth century that the medium truly took hold on the Continent. The first known woodcut — depicting Buddha in a Chinese manuscript — is said to have been executed in A.D. 868, but among the earliest examples known today are a *Madonna with Four Virgin Saints in a Garden*, believed to have been carved in 1418 (Bibliothèque Royale, Brussels), and a German *St. Christopher*, pulled in the year 1423 (John Rylands Library, Manchester). The woodcut, particularly renditions of Biblical themes, flourished in both France and Germany during this period. These prints were soon prevalent in Austria, Bohemia, Bavaria, and other areas of Europe.

By the mid-fifteenth century, crude but usable playing cards were being produced with the woodcut technique. But this era heralded a development of greater significance: the invention of movable type. At this time, entire pages of books — illustrations as well as text — were carved and reproduced through the woodcut method. Known as "block-book" printing, the technique is believed to have originated in the Netherlands in 1470; it was still in practice in Rome in 1548. Whether or not the painstaking block-book carving of text stimulated the invention of movable type (which, of course, was reusable) has been debated. What cannot be denied is that block-book printing thrived during the period: beautifully illustrated religious volumes produced in Florence and Venice testify to this.

By the sixteenth century the popularity of the woodcut had reached full fruition through the work of Albrecht Dürer. Born in Nuremberg in 1471. Dürer was apprenticed for three years to the painter Michael Wolgemut, whose workshop produced many of the woodcut illustrations for books of that time.

Dürer's contribution to the medium was both prolific and dynamic: not only did he encourage other artists throughout Europe toward perfecting the technique, but his influence was felt in the adaptation of subject matter other than religion, including politics, comment on social movements of the time, caricature, cartooning, and criticism.

Under patronage of Emperor Maximilian, many ambitious book illustration projects were initiated. Thus encouraged, Dürer and others (including Hans Holbein the Younger and Lucas van Leyden in Germany and Campagnola and de' Barbari in Italy) continued their efforts in developing the woodcut toward a medium of mass appeal and acceptance.

Dürer died in the year 1528. Two decades later, with the advent of line engraving and etching reproduction, the popularity of the woodcut medium declined sharply. Some 200 years were to pass before it would flourish again.

A woodcut of 1756 that served as a business card for a pin manufacturing company.

Madonna with Four Virgin Saints in a Garden. Originating in the year 1418 and considered one of the earliest known woodcuts.

Prelum Ascesianu

13

aber dise ding fleissiger wissen wolt der mag die auß dem prunnen schöpffen vnnd mer dañ wir in disem buch begreiffen mügen wunderperlicher ding suchen.vnd weñ nw solche zerstrewung auff dem ertreich beschiht. vnd der almechtig komen wirdt in dem stul vnd thron seiner maiestat alle selen vnd die gantzen werlt zerichten so wirdt in derselben zeit ein offenbare gemayne vrstend aller menschen.alßdeñ wirdt der leichnam der do auff ersteet von den todten vnzerstörlich vnd vntödlich.nicht allain der gerechten sunder auch der sünder.doch der gerechten das sie alweg bey Cristo bleybē mügē.aber der sünder das sie on ir vergencknus verschuldte straff vnd peyn leyden.zu letst wirdt der gerecht richter die gerechten mit ewigkeit der glori begaben.vnnd den vn guetigen lange schmah vnd peyn auflegen.derselben leichname werden in ewigkeit bleiben zu geduldung ewi ger creutzigung.marter vnd peyn des fewrs.das vil anders genaturt ist dañ das vnßer.das doch wo es mit ei nicher materi nicht enthalten würdt erlischet.aber ihens ewig fewr lebt vnd schwebt durchsichselbs alweg on einiche materliche ernerung vnd gibt ime selbs ewige fürung vñ enthaltung vñ bringt peylichkeit des schmertz ens.Was vnaußsprechenlicher freud vnd frolockung werden aber die gerechten vnd guetigeu habē so sie nach empfliehung des ewigen iamers.ellends vnd quals zu disem gerechsten richter vnd allergüetigisten vater tret ten vnd rue für arbait.das leben für den tod.die klarheit für die finsternus.die ewigen vñ himlische güetere für die irdischen vnd kurtzen empfahen werden.darumb sollen alle menschen fleiß an keren sich auff das schierst zu dem rechten weg zeschicken oder in angenomner vbung der tugent vnd in volbringung des arbaitsamen lebes gedultigclich zebeharren vnd also göttlichs trosts vnd lons zeerwarten.dañ vnßer vater vnd herr(der den hi mel gezymert vnd befesstigt.die sunnen mit anderm gestirne erleuchtet.das ertreich mit bergen vmbfangen.mit dem meer vmbgeben.vnd mit wasserflüßen vnderschaiden.vnd alle ding in diser werlt auß nichtē beschaffen hat)der hat auch in betrachtung der irrung der menschen vns einen füerer layter vnd anweiser auff den weg 8 gerechtigkeit gesendet.dem wöllen wir alle nachfolgen.den wöllen wir hören.dem wöllen wir fleißigclich vñ andechtigclich gehorsam sein vnd wöllen mit dem alten feind des menschlichen hayls(deñ wir kennen)manlich lich vnd kunlich in den kampff tretten vnd nach vberwindung desselben vnßers widersachers triumphirende vnd obsigende der versprochen belonung der tugent von got vnzweifellich gewarten vnd durch die grossen pforten vber den gestirntē himel auff in den höhsten himel eingeen.Alda dañ die statt der selligen burgere vnd gottes vnßer müter Jherusalem in den mytteln feldern des hymels erscheinen wirdt.Dise statt gottes hat ein liecht gleich eim costenlichen stayn.Ir mawr ist gros vnd hoh mit.xij.pforten.vnd geschriben namē der.xij.ge schlecht der kinder israhel.vier seyten.als do sinnd die vier tayl der werlt.die mawr der statt die do vieregket ist hat.xij.grundfest vnd dariñ die.xij.namen der.xij.appostel.vnd die grundfest der mawr der statt sinnd mit allē köstliche stayn geziert.darumb weñ wir in diss war vaterland wider eingeen so werden wir mit vnaußsprech licher freud iubel vnd frolockung durchgossen.in welchem vaterland wir entsprungen vnd darauß pürtig sind O wie werden wir frolocken so wir nach disem langem iamerigem vnd geferlichem ellend vnßer freudēreichs vaterland ewiger seligkeit glori vnd ere anplicken vnd sehen werden.darumb sollen wir bittē das der herr vns vnd allen den die diss hörē verleyhe mit bewartem von vns empfangnem glawben nach verscheynung 8 zeit der hinderlegtē vnd berayten kron der gerechtigkeit zeerharren.vnd vnder den ihenen die in das ewig lebē auff ersteen gefunden vnd von ewiger schand vnnd peyn geledigt zewerden durch Jhesum cristum vnßern herrñ. durch den sey got vater dem almechtigen mit dem heilligen gaist ewigs lob.ere.benedeyūg.preys.klarheit.weiß heit.gewalt.hayl.kraft.tugent vnd glori zu ewiger danckperkeit gesagt in die ewigkeit der ewigkeit Amen.

Illustrations from the famous Nuremberg Chronicle are depicted on page 15, and on pages 16 and 17. Published in 1493, the Nuremberg Chronicle paralleled the Gutenberg Bible in importance. It was a richly illustrated world history which firmly established Nuremberg as the center of printing craftsmanship in that era. Its more than 2,000 woodcuts depicting figures and magnificent views of cities were marked by strong individual treatment, perspective, and originality. Published by Anton Koberger and featuring woodcuts by Pleydenwuff and Wolgemut, it was the most commanding book of the fifteenth century. It is interesting to note that Albrecht Dürer for a time studied and worked in Wolgemut's studio.

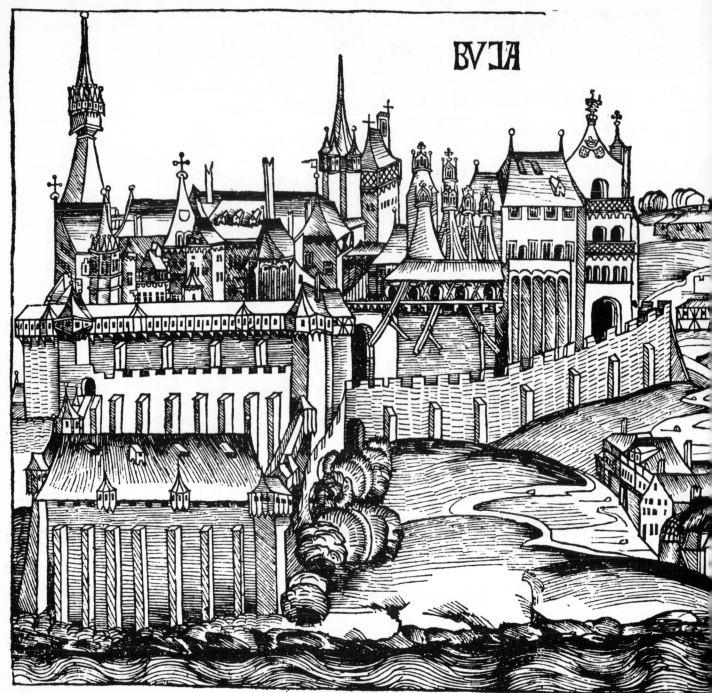

BVIA

Aries (The Ram), from a book published in Venice in 1485 by C. J. Hyginus. (Reproduced courtesy Victoria and Albert Museum, London.)

Opposite Page

The king and queen of cups from an eighteenth century deck of tarot cards produced from woodcuts. Playing cards manufactured through this process were most often hand colored.

Woodcut initials by Jean Michel Papillon, first shown in Paris in 1760. The son of a famous fine wallpaper manufacturer, Papillon was among the first artists to attempt decorative illustration of an image within the individual woodcut initial.

Top Right. An illustration from the German best seller of the 1600s, *Ship of Fools*. The artist has used his knife as if it were a brush to create an extremely fine line.

Below. Woodcut illustration by Hokusai, Japan's famous pioneer woodcut artist (1760-1849). (Reproduced courtesy Stanley Lewis, Montreal.)

Opposite Page

Le Tzar Alexandre de Macédoine, a 1750 Russian woodcut illustration.

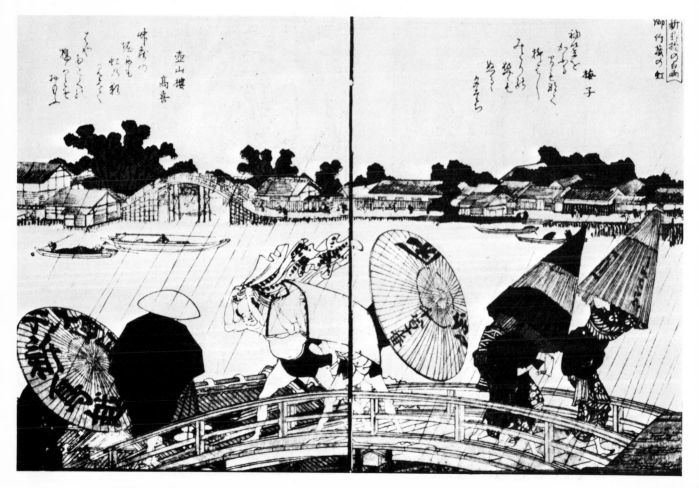

ЦРЬ АЛЕѴАНДРЪ МАКЕДОНСКИ:

Macbeth, Banquo and the Three Witches, a sixteenth century illustration from *Chronicles of England, Scotland and Ireland* by Raphael Holinshed. (Reproduced courtesy the British Museum, London.) Using wood in each instance, the artist has brought out characteristics of his own regional environment.

Mr. Richard Mather.
This woodcut by John
Foster (1670) is the
oldest surviving American
print. Conscious of the
grain of the wood, the
artist used it as a vital
part of the print's
composition. (Reproduced
by arrangement with the
American Antiquarian
Society, Worcester,
Mass.)

2.
The Woodcut in America

The first known American woodcut is the 1670 portrait of Richard Mather attributed to John Foster, America's first engraver and pioneer printer. Other woodcuts followed at a sporadic pace until the time of Alexander Anderson, who, through his work in wood engraving beginning in 1795, started to formulate and evolve a national American approach to the medium.

Anderson was greatly influenced by England's Thomas Bewick, who at that time was executing animals, birds, and outdoor scenes of great charm and beauty through the method known as the white line wood engraving.

Until Bewick's time, the most accepted method of working in woodcut was to draw the composition or design on a block of wood and then with a knife (and other sharp or specially shaped instruments conceived for woodcutting) to cut away the surrounding areas of the wood surface between the drawn lines. When inked and pressed against paper, the

drawing (which was the raised, untouched portion of the surface) captured the ink and reproduced in the form of a black line against a white background. Usually these were cut in the direction of — or with — the grain. Though this facilitated the physical cutting process, it often softened the line of the work because cutting along the grain made it susceptible to wear, shredding, and splitting under use.

Bewick and others pioneered in the opposite direction. Using the hard end or cross-grained surface of the wood, the design was engraved with a burin or sharp-edged cutting tool. When processed, the background caught the ink and printed black on the paper; the design or engraved composition — not catching any of the ink — reproduced as white lines. This method came to be known as the wood engraving or the white-line woodcut.

America had a number of woodcut artists prior to Anderson. Among these

were Thomas Smith, who carved decorative floral borders for bookplates in 1707; Titan and Felix Leeds, whose woodcuts served as title pages for a number of almanacs published in New York and Philadelphia at the turn of the century; James Franklin (a brother to Benjamin Franklin), whose work appeared on book frontispieces from 1717 to 1719; Christopher Sower, Justin Fox, Henry Dawkins, Benjamin Keach, and Peter Maverick. With varying degrees of recognition, their work in the medium became known through the almanacs, school books, song books, social commentaries and recitations published during the period. Frequently woodcuts used for reproduction in these publications were the unsigned carvings of print-shop workmen; it wasn't until the beginning of the nineteenth century that the medium attained a full sense of professionalism.

Beginning with the work and time of

Hall (both pupils of Anderson), William Williams, William Mason, Abel Bowen, Anderson, American artists began to show a unique talent for woodcutting and wood engraving. Encouraged by commissions from periodicals such as *The Family Magazine* and *Harper's Weekly*, and stimulated by a budding book industry requiring numerous illustrations, a number of artists achieved prominence in the medium. Anderson illustrated books such as *The Vicar of Wakefield, A General History of Quadrupeds,* and *The Fables of Flora,* all published in the early 1800s. Other woodcut illustrators of the period included Garret Lansing and John H.

John W. Barber, Benson Lossing, G. T. Devereux, W. J. Linton, Winslow Homer, Felix Darley, William Croome, Henry Marsh, and many others (by 1870 some 400 artists were working professionally in the field), most of whom employed the Bewick white-line technique.

At this time, too, the wood-block technique was being used to print huge circus and other posters which found their way throughout America and Europe. Conceived by print shop craftsmen of Germanic origin, these left little to the imagination and depicted their story in a curt and blunt manner.

In 1875, a new breed of woodcut and

wood engraving artist emerged on the American scene, coinciding with the rapid development of photo-mechanical techniques that were to revolutionize the printing industry. Compositions and studies pulled from wood were issued in a series of portfolios. No longer illustrations to be accompanied or deluged by text and printed explanation, they stood on their own as legitimate works of art. The movement was known as the Society of American Engravers, headed by a talented wood engraving artist named Timothy Cole.

The woodcut was emerging from a medium of illustration and reportage to become a viable and recognized art form.

Opposite Page

Woodcut almanac illustration from
Handbook of Early Advertising Art.
(Published by Dover Publications,
Inc.)

Woodcut illustration from an early
spelling book. (Reproduced from *Old
Time Schools and School-books* by
Clifton Johnson. Published by Dover
Publications, Inc.)

Newspaper display with woodcut pictorial illustrations. This advertisement from the Philadelphia Chronicle, April 27, 1831, is one example of the variety of stock woodcuts available from the time of Benjamin Franklin. Philadelphia newspapers pioneered in the use of stock woodcuts for advertising purposes. (Reproduced from *Handbook of Early Advertising Art.* Published by Dover Publications, Inc.)

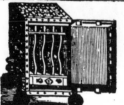

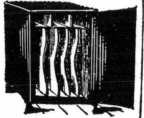

Early nineteenth century woodcut poster with typographic border ornaments by J. H. Coach and transportation lines were among the leading poster and newspaper advertisers in pioneer America. (Reproduced courtesy the Landauer Collection, from Handbook of Early Advertising Art. Published by Dover Publications, Inc.)

TROY, BALLSTON
AND
SARATOGA,

DAILY LINE OF
COACHES.

This line will commence running on the first day of July, leaving each place at half past 8 A. M. every day. Passengers wishing to travel from Saratoga to Lebanon Springs, will find this line not only the most expeditious but cheapest.

Passengers for Pittsfield, Northampton and Hartford by taking this line will dine at Troy, lodge at Pittsfield, and arrive at Hartford early the next day. The road is now put in the best order, and all that is now wanting is that liberality which the establishment merits.

☞ *Seats taken at G. W. Wilcox's*, York House, *Saratoga*, and at all the Principal Houses in Troy.

L. V. & J. B. REED, Proprietors.
J. S. KEELER, *Agent*, Troy.
S. DEXTER, *Agent*, Saratoga.

TROY, JUNE 25, 1834.

N. B. On the arrival of the ERIE or CHAMPLAIN, Parties can be accommodated with coaches to Saratoga or Ballston the same evening.

An illustration of *Pullman Vestibuled Cars*. Many of the illustrations for railway advertising from 1850 to 1900 were produced through the wood engraving medium.

Woodcut illustrations from *The Picture Alphabet Book of 1830*. The treatment in these early schoolbooks was light and simple for easy comprehension. (Published by the American Review, Scotia, N.Y.)

N

Was the Nest which, last week, our Charles
Brought home in his hat from the wood;
'Twas cruel, papa said, the young ones to take,
No boy would do so, who was good.

Easy words of three letters.

Bed [2]	Cat [2]	Hat [2]
Bee [1]	Hen [2]	Mug [2]
Fly [1]	Pig [2]	Sun [2]
Bat [2]	Rat [2]	Leg [2]
Bug [2]	Cup [2]	Tub [2]
Fox [5]	Cap [2]	Gun [2]

Illustrations from *The Little Reader's Assistant*, published in 1790 by Webster. *Above, left. Story of Columbus.* Note how the haphazard chipping technique conveys the feeling of waves. *Above, right. Putnam and the Wolf.* The field and land areas have been emphasized by light scratchings on the wood. *Below, left. Night Attack of Indians on Major Waldron's House, Dover, N. H.* The starkness of the parallel lines, white Indians and black background all contribute to the strength of the composition. *Below, right. A Christian Getting the Best of a Heathen Indian.* A very few lines seem to make the rocks monumental. These four illustrations have different borders; similarly, the techniques used in each composition vary to create entirely different results.

Opposite Page

John Rogers Being Burned at the Stake. Woodcut illustration from *A Rude Primer.*

3.
A Modern Art Form

Thomas Bewick, whose beautiful white-line illustrations of the world of nature revived woodcut and wood engraving printing, was a great influence on the artists of his era. In England, William Blake and others were to follow in this technique; in France, a new age of wood engraving came into being with the romantic volume or book, richly illustrated by artists such as Doré, Johannt, Gavarni, Monnier, and Meissonier.

Important to the development of the woodcut as a modern art influence is the prolific work of Katsushika Hokusai. In his lifetime (1760-1849), this great Japanese artist produced some 30,000 compositions — a good many of them under pseudonyms, a Japanese practice of the time.

During his 90 years of life, Hokusai — through single and multi-colored woodcuts and wood engravings — depicted many aspects of Japan: its natural beauty, the good or rigorous life of its people, their religious and philosophical beliefs. As an illustrator of both literature and life, he was known to be restless, dissatisfied, and (as he once wrote) seeking the time when ". . . every line and dot I draw will be imbued with life . . ." Hokusai gave the woodcut and wood block print scope and flexibility. His compositions have served for students in all media as virtual manuals in the study of purity and forcefulness of line, rhythm, and the use of space.

By the mid-eighteenth century, the black-line method of woodcut illustration was being popularized in England by the Dalziel brothers; but, with the rapid development of photo-mechanical means of reproduction, this revival was short-lived. Simultaneous with developments in America, the English woodcut was moving from a medium used basically for illustration to an independent form of artistic expression.

Perhaps the first artist of major importance to steer it in this direction was Paul Gauguin; in 1894 Gauguin returned to France from his Tahitian adventure with ten wood block two-tone color compositions. Though the techniques Gauguin used for this work were interesting and complex, of greater importance is the impetus he gave the medium by initiating an awareness of its full potentialities. Other great artists in Europe, America, and the Far East were to explore further and find permanent expression through the woodcut and wood engraving. These included Edvard Munch, who was able to derive a forceful and haunting style through the nature of the wood itself; Ernst Ludwig Kirchner, Emil Nolde,

Christian Rohlfs, and others of this era. They explored the basic essentials of wood, producing prints of great strength or sensitivity, as the case might be, but always of vitality.

During the 1920s and 1930s the woodcut and wood engraving medium was kept vigorous in the United States by artists such as Rockwell Kent, Eric Gill, and Thomas Nason. In Japan, Shiko Munakata's powerful wood block prints, influenced by the folklore and Buddhist belief of his people, began to emerge; by mid-century, they were to achieve a unique position of universal artistic influence. By the mid '40s and early '50s, Misch Kohn, Antonio Frasconi, Leonard Baskin, and other artists in America were giving the woodcut and wood engraving new direction and impetus, which have influenced seriously still other young artists in the medium.

This section indicates something of the success of twentieth-century artists in the medium and discusses some of the techniques they have employed. Because of space limitations, it is not possible to depict the interesting and notable compositions of many others working in this field today. Still, the following pages represent a worthy cross-section of an art form which again pulsates with challenge and potentiality.

Zuerichsee by Ernst Ludwig Kirchner (1880-1938. There is a great deal of activity reflected in the woodcut by Kirchner, a leader of the Expressionist movement of his day. One sees boats, a steamship, fishermen, canoes and rowboats. The water is alive and all the action appears to be coming toward the viewer. The procession of people going back and forth across the bridge increases the action.

Above, left. Self-portrait by Käthe Kollwitz, 1923. *Above, right.* Selbstildnis (self-portrait) by Max Beckmann, 1922. *Below, left. Hugo Biallowons* by Ernst Ludwig Kirchner, 1916. *Below, right. Baertiger Mann* by Erich Heckel, 1908. It is interesting to compare the composition techniques employed by these foremost German woodcut artists. Beckmann has isolated the face in order to give it strength, while the Kollwitz face is buried in the black so that it appears to emerge from and yet, at the same time, be swallowed by it. Kirchner has used black to give the face greater drama; Heckel, on the contrary, achieves his dramatic effect by using a great deal of white in his composition. The irregular lettering in the Kirchner woodcut appears to be a product of the woodcutting process and readily becomes a part of the overall design.

Above. Das Tor, 1920. *Opposite page.*
Kirche, 1921. Two woodcuts by Lyonel
Feininger. Both compositions are
identical in size and subject matter, but
they are completely opposite in feeling
because of the amount of wood that has
or has not been cut away. One print is
predominantly white, the other
overwhelmingly black, yet both are
equally strong in visual impact.

49

Opposite Page

Above, left. Lichterkopf by Emile Nolde.
Below, left. Frauenkopf by Karl
Schmidt-Rottluf. *Right. Portrait of
Ludwig Schamer* by Ernst Ludwig
Kirchner, 1918. (Reproduced courtesy
Dr. and Mrs. Ernst Fischer, Albany,

N.Y.) In the Nolde woodcut the swirl
of the hair and the round form give the
girl a somewhat frivolous character,
while angular lines make the
Schmidt-Rottluff head very serious.
Kirchner uses a multiplicity of fine
lines and a scratchy effect to give his
work a feeling of age.

Way to Emmaus by Karl
Schmidt-Rottluff. The three figures are
identical except for the heads, on which
the artist has placed much emphasis.
There are many Expressionist facets to
this woodcut; among them the road and
the sphere, which simultaneously appear
to be moving in opposite directions.
(Reproduced courtesy of Philadelphia
Museum of Art. Photo by A. J. Wyatt.)

Right. Dancing Figures.
Opposite page. A selection of illustrations. Woodcut compositions by Emile Nolde. In the marvelous *Dancing Figures* woodcut essay, all the people appear to be dancing in a different manner (twirling, flying around, and jumping) because of the way in which the wood was cut. Compare this to the woodcuts above in which the heavy framing seems to have stopped the action and the viewer must look inside the frame to get the sense of the subject matter. Again, with very few cuts in the wood, the artist has made it possible for strong figures to emerge. Nolde's stamp size compositions seem to have been done quickly, almost like a doodle, and one has the feeling they are preliminary to a more important work to come.

LA DANSE

54

La Danse by Raoul Dufy, 1912. This is a very elegant woodcut in which the figures intertwine with each other and the background so that the entire composition appears to be one. Not only are the figures dancing, but the environment is dancing along with them. A hole has been cut into the composition to introduce an oncoming ship in the distance; this tends to give depth to the entire woodcut.

Illustration from the *Kegon Sutra Suite* by Shiko Munakata, 1937. Here we also see a dance, but it is a dance of nature. This Munakata composition looks almost as if a very small portion of the Dufy woodcut had been isolated and enlarged. This woodcut has the quality of a drawing created with black ink dropped onto paper. (Reproduced courtesy Kodansha, Tokyo.)

Reeds by Shiko Munakata, 1955.
Munakata is considered the greatest
contemporary Japanese woodcut artist.
His powerful prints, for the most part
in black and white, have been
acclaimed at exhibitions throughout the
world. Munakata's work has brought
new vitality and inspiration to one of
Japan's most traditional art forms. He
is a religious man, and much of his
subject matter has embraced the Zen
philosophy. (Reproduced courtesy
Kodansha, Tokyo.)

Horse by Jacob Pins. The horse,
skillfully portrayed in a most difficult
position, is coming right at the viewer.
This composition is Munch-like because
of its heavy, black principal figure. A
sense of drama is achieved by the
vertical lines; without them the
composition would lose much of its
effect.

Flower Hunting Mural by Shiko Munakata, 1957. In his book *The Story of Wood Prints*, this famous Japanese artist wrote "I advise the layman to spread India ink on an uncarved board, lay paper on top of it and (to) print it. He will get a black print, but the result is not the blackness of the ink; it is the blackness of prints. Whatever I carve, I compare to the uncarved print and ask myself: which has more beauty . . . strength . . . depth . . . magnitude . . . tranquility . . . ? If there is anything that is inferior to an uncarved block, then I have not created my print. I have lost to the board." (Reproduced courtesy Kodansha, Tokyo.)

Opposite Page

Above, left. Singing Rye by Gunar Krolis. *Below, left. Departure* by Stanley Lewis (Canada). *Right. Old City of Jerusalem* by Jacob Steinhardt (Israel).

Corridor of Katsura Kyoto by Un-ichi Kiratsuka, 1966 (Japan). The woodcuts on these two pages were printed in one color in different localities throughout the world. The techniques employed portray something of the environment, beliefs, and cultures involved.

Self-Portrait by Leonard Baskin, 1963. Baskin, a printmaker and sculptor, has mastered the wood engraving technique; much of his work in this medium has been monumental in size as well as in subject matter. (Reproduced courtesy the Kovler Gallery, Chicago.)

Thinking Man by Steven Trefonides. The shape of the wood has created the figure, while large areas of the composition were left untouched and unincised. Details were added to accentuate the face, hands, and feet.

The '30s, an illustration by Seymour Chwast for *Push Pin Graphics, No. 36*. An elegant board meeting in a hotel suite. The stark figures are crowded into the center of the work, while at its extremities abstract patterns of ferns and mosaic flooring arrest the viewer's attention. The table of Eastern design serves as a visual break between the hulking figures and the fine details at the room's perimeter. (Reproduced courtesy Push Pin Studios, Inc., New York.)

Above. Clam Diggers by Antonio Frasconi, 1954. Like Baskin, Antonio Frasconi, who came to the U.S. from Uruguay in the 1940s, is responsible for the revival of the woodcut medium in America. His work takes full advantage of the texture and character of wood and has inspired young artists to work in and master the medium. In this woodcut, the poles in the background are heavy, strong, and domineering, while the men in the foreground appear to be lost between the sea and the height of the piece. The viewer gains the immediate impression that clam digging is hard work. (Reproduced courtesy the Fogg Art Museum, Harvard University. Gift of Meta and Paul Sachs.)

Below. Happening by Jacob Landau. In this woodcut, Landau, who works in many media, has depicted a large group of figures dancing, running, and moving in many different directions. Some of the figures are short; others are elongated and out of proportion to their sense of motion and direction. In other instances, the figures appear to be shadows of each other. To emphasize movement in a number of directions, the wood has been cut away around the arms and legs of the figures.

66

Jacob No. 2 by Emil Mirk. This detail from a very large woodcut depicts a head and eye which seem to be peeking out of the wood and appear to have come about by using a wide, flat tool to incise the wood surface. There is quite a contrast between the very wide and extremely fine lines. Because of their proximity to each other, the wide lines seem larger, while the fine lines seem smaller than they actually are. This contrast and that of large areas of white and black beside each other give the viewer an impression of much activity and movement. (Photo by Richard Braaten.)

Woodcut by Misch Kohn. The artist has given deliberate thought to the placement and execution of each line and every dot. Each black and white area plays against the other; the overall effect is that of a fully planned and very serious wood engraving composition.

Woodcut composition by Dan Fruits. The artist has given his work a spirit of lightness by attempting to retain characteristics of the wood which might contribute toward the overall expression of a forest growing. The top of the woods appears to be reaching skyward, while the trees in the foreground seem to have an inner growth. The artist chipped away the wood in an almost accidental fashion to ronder a quick, impromptu impression.

Wood-type composite collage by Murray Tinkelman. The artist has used actual wood block type faces — most of them carved by hand from hard cherry wood — to form an assemblage of letters. These were glued onto a piece of plywood which was then cut into a circle four feet in diameter. A print could be pulled from this low relief, mammoth woodcut of letters.

4.
Projects and Demonstrations

This chapter provides step-by-step procedures and techniques for carrying out a number of woodcut print projects.

The traditional form of carving a woodcut and printing from it is demonstrated by artist Bill Greer, who uses two squares of pine to produce a floral composition of appeal and sensitivity.

Norman Laliberté demonstrates a number of woodcut techniques working in pine, Masonite, and plywood, illustrating both flexibility in the use of wood and paper materials and spontaneity in working with manual and power tools.

A number of points should be kept in mind when carrying out projects such as these:

Preliminary drawings: these should be sketchy; their purpose should be to provide guidance and general definition to the drawing rather than exact cutting lines. (In the traditional woodcut procedure, as demonstrated by Bill Greer, detailed drawing *is* necessary.)

Tools: these should be used with dexterity and a spirit of freedom. Safety, however, should always be a key factor. Use bits and cutting instruments as you would a pencil. Remember that cutting tools or rotary bits have different impressions. Be selective according to the line required.

Paper: experiment! Use a variety of papers in an array of colors; different weights and textures of paper yield interesting results.

Inks: remember that there are a multitude of printing inks in addition to black.

Wood: use the other side of your pine block and relate it to your original composition. Pick interesting shapes and pieces off the workshop floor; these present unusual hand-stamping potential.

The finished print: this need not be the end, but rather the beginning. Multiple image and overlapping can add vitality to a print. Graphic elements within a print can be cut or torn from their environment and reassembled elsewhere to form the basis of a new work of art, to be enlarged or embellished in other media. Intact, any print can be given effervescence and enlargement by continuing to work on it with pastels, oil crayons, color pencils, chalks and dyes. Papers colored with pastels or other media before they are applied to the ink block yield interesting and unusual effects. A finished print, while still wet, can be sprinkled with metallic powder to completely transform the composition and bring it new brilliance. In essence, the print need not be the end, but rather — with experimentation — it can be the beginning and inspiration for a unique and highly individual work of art.

A number of finished compositions by Norman Laliberté, on paper, cloth, and fabric produced from pine, Masonite and plywood, complete the chapter.

All photographs in the Projects and Demonstrations by Richard Braaten.

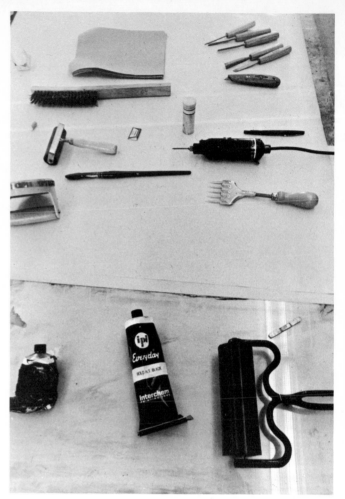

1. and 2.   Photographed are the various tools and materials used in this woodcut demonstration by artist Bill Greer. Included are nails of varying sizes and thicknesses, hard wire brushes, an ice pick, razor blades, various mechanical and woodcutting hand tools, rollers, and a selection of papers of different quality, weight, color and texture.

3. The artist makes his preliminary sketch or drawing on a piece of paper.

4. The boards for a diptych (two piece) composition are cut from a piece of pine. The boards are clear-grained and without knots.

5. The drawing is made directly on the board with a Pentel pen. A brush and ink can also be used for this purpose. The blacked in or drawn areas will remain uncut and therefore will reproduce when inked.

6. Another method of delineating the drawing is to paint the entire surface of the block with black ink. When dry, the design or composition is drawn over the black with chalk. This gives the artist a better idea of the character of the finished woodcut, since in this method the white or chalked areas are cut away. Cutting is done in the direction away from the artist and against a stationery piece of wood which absorbs the motion of the cut while keeping the woodcut block in place.

7. Cutting out larger sections of the wood.

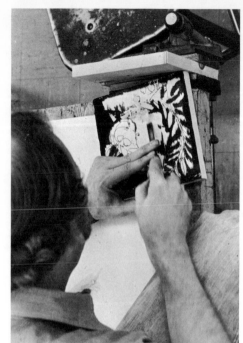

8. Cutting is done along the grain of the wood. If the composition has a border, care must be taken to arrest the pressure of the cut before the edge hits the area to remain intact.

9. Bill Greer varies the tools in accordance with the nature of the cut that is required: coarse instruments are available for gouging large areas of wood; very fine tools are used for cutting more intricate details. Pine is a soft wood, and therefore, all tools must be sharp.

The tools used vary in accordance with the character of the detail being cut. For instance, a very fine instrument is used to delineate the stem of a flower, while a broader knife gives definition to the nature or substance of a leaf. In itself, the block is a composition of beauty with its carving and hollows of varying depth and the imprint of the different tools. Much of this beauty, of course, will not register on the print because it exists below the printing surface. Fine detail in the composition is added with nail point and razor blade scratching and etching.

13. The blocks are inked with a roller.

14. Paper is placed over the blocks and rubbed with a clean roller.

15. The paper may also be rubbed by hand with a cloth.

16. The woodcut print is pulled from the blocks.

17. The carved wood blocks and the print which they produced.

The blocks can be printed in almost any color on different kinds and weights of paper as well as on unusually textured and colored paper stocks. Interesting prints can also be made on fabrics and cloth. Multiple images, over-prints and double exposures are all possible because the blocks can be inked and handled with comparative ease.

Photographed are the
various bits and electric rotary
tools used by Norman Laliberté
in the projects and
demonstrations which follow.

Pine Board Project

1. A drawing of a young girl's
head is made with ink and brush
on a 10 or 12 inch wide piece of
pine board. The free and flowing
sketch is used as a general guide
for cutting and incision.

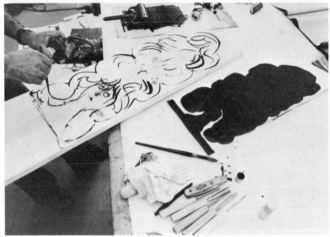

2. The head is shaped and
defined in outline form through
the use of an electric band saw.

3. and 4.   More detail is shaped into the general outline of the head by means of the band saw. The saw, in a way, is almost like a pencil, providing greater definition to the circumference of the composition.

5.   Using the rotary and different bits and cutting tools, incisions of varying depth and width are cut into the surface of the pine board to delineate eyes, mouth, nose, etc., falls of hair and other facial detail.

6. The various bits and cutting edges are used like a pencil to incise more detail and character into the composition. Decorative elements are also added in this manner.

7. The wood surface is sandpapered and wire brushed to clean out all sawdust from the lines and crevices. Texture can be added at this point, if desired, by the pressure and motion of the abrasive or brush.

8. The wood surface is inked. Care is taken to distribute the ink evenly over the entire area.

9. A sheet of paper is placed over the inked wood. The paper can be pressed by hand and cloth or with a roller.

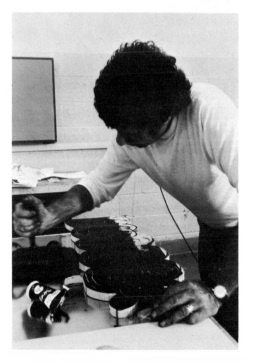

 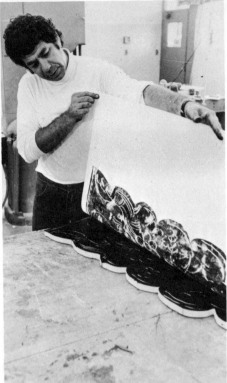 

10.   Additional lines may be added to the individual print by drawing with a blunt instrument over the paper before it is pulled away from the inked block. Any pressure on top of the paper at this point will produce an exact white area or line as in the monoprinting technique. These lines make no impression on the wood block, but do give an individual touch to each print.

11. and 12.   The print is pulled from the wood block.

At this point, the artist has a number of alternatives. If not completely satisfied with his result, he may choose to cut more detail or decorative elements into the wood block, then pulling a new print. Or the print itself can be cut into a new shape or composition and, while still wet, applied to the surface of a clean board, thus producing an entirely new drawing from which to make a second woodcut. In this instance, the artist chose to reverse the piece of pine and, within its existing shape or circumference, embarked on an entirely new composition from which another print was pulled. The results appear on the following pages.

The original woodcut
print pulled from the pine
board: the head of a
young girl.

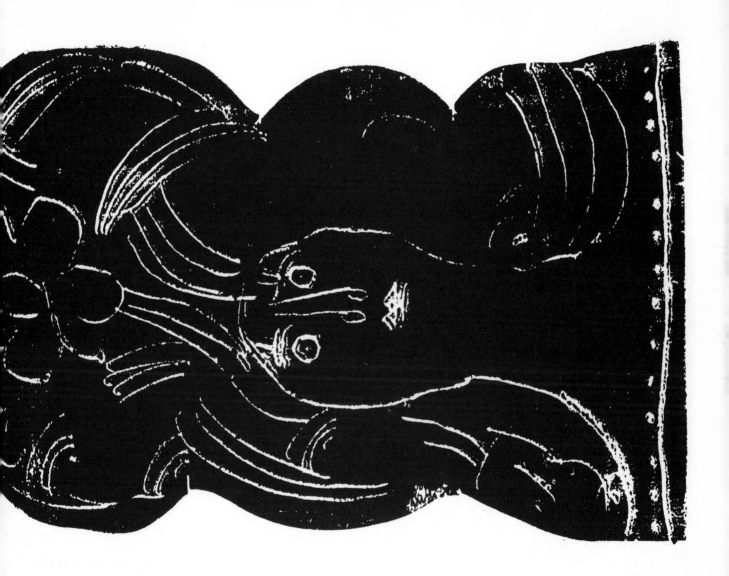

83

The reverse side of the
original pine wood block:
a new composition — a
bearded old man — has
been cut into the same
circumference which
formed the outline of the
young girl. The
composition is called
"Susannah and the
Elders."

84

13. Wooden hand printing blocks can be made with power tools. Cutting and incising techniques, as employed in the previous project, are used.

14. As with the head project, the reverse side of the block can be used to create new compositions for hand-stamping possibilities.

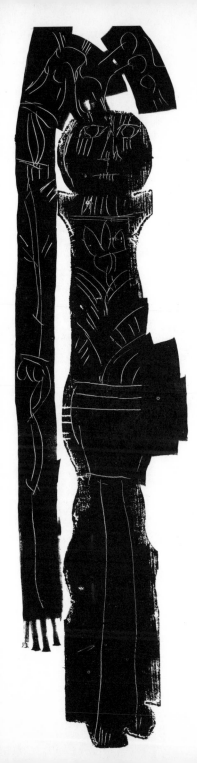

This doll print was produced in the hand stamping technique. A rough outline of a doll was first sketched in negative with brushed ink on a 3 inch plank. The band was then used almost as a drawing instrument to determine the exact outline of the doll. Decorative and feature details were cut into the surface by using a variety of rotary bits almost as if they were pencils of various sizes and densities. Cross-hatch strokes were cut into the background areas which could not be cut away and therefore would reproduce in the print, while deep-cutting bits eliminated areas not to appear in the printed compositions. Fine detail was added with sharp nail scratching. The surface was brushed and sandpapered, then inked. Printing and hand-stamping were made on papers of varying weights, colors and textures.

15. In the "multiples" project which follows, individual parts or elements — a vase, a flower, leaves, a stem, the sun — are drawn onto wood with a pentel pen and cut out with a band saw. The drawing serves as a general guide and the saw does not follow it precisely. In this way, wood pieces develop their own individual character.

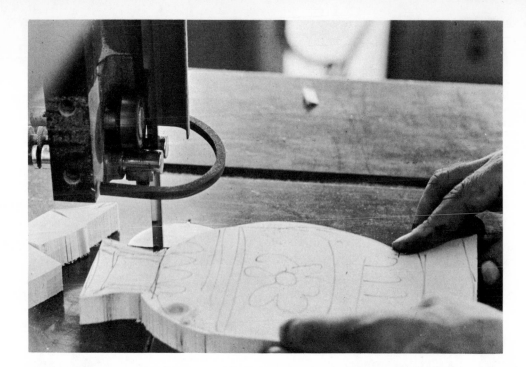

16. Rotary bits are used to incise details into the individual parts and pieces.

The techniques and methods employed in the previous two demonstrations are used in this multiples project. The only difference is that, unlike the head and doll compositions, the elements here are individual, they are not united at this point within one overall composition.

17. Fine details are inscribed into each piece with a sharp nail. They are cleaned of sawdust with a steel brush and inked individually with a roller.

A composition is hand-stamped on paper of various kinds and colors. Decorative touches or motifs can be added by picking up found triangles, squares and rectangles from the workshop floor; sanding, then using them in hand-stamp fashion.

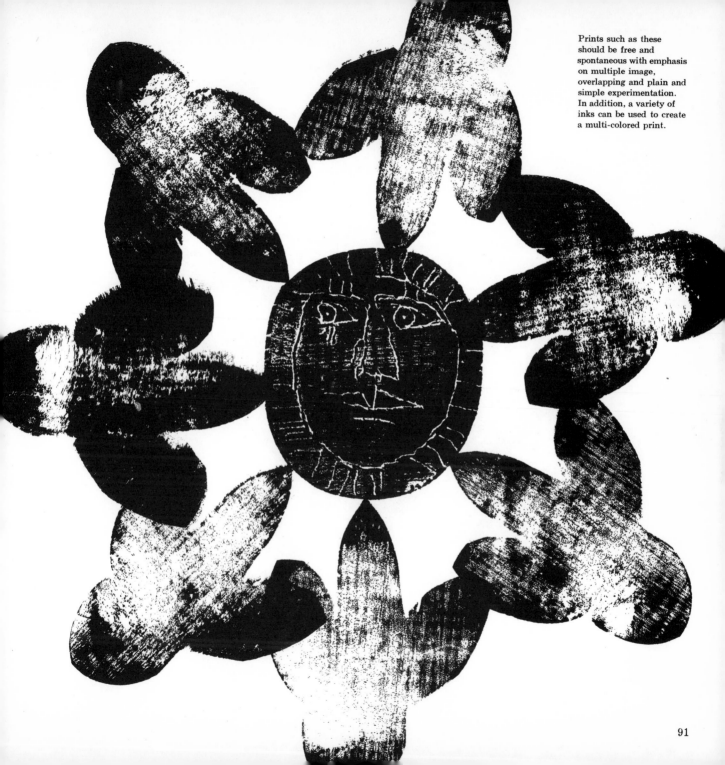

Prints such as these should be free and spontaneous with emphasis on multiple image, overlapping and plain and simple experimentation. In addition, a variety of inks can be used to create a multi-colored print.

93

Using the same hand-stamping elements, partial graphics are printed, to be completed by Pentel or ink and brush extentions or elaborations. Many graphic elements within the finished woodcut prints can be cut, torn or ripped out of their environment and reassembled and reshaped on a fresh piece of paper to form the nucleus or inspiration for a new composition to be completed by drawing in colored inks, or with crayons, pencils, paint or watercolors.

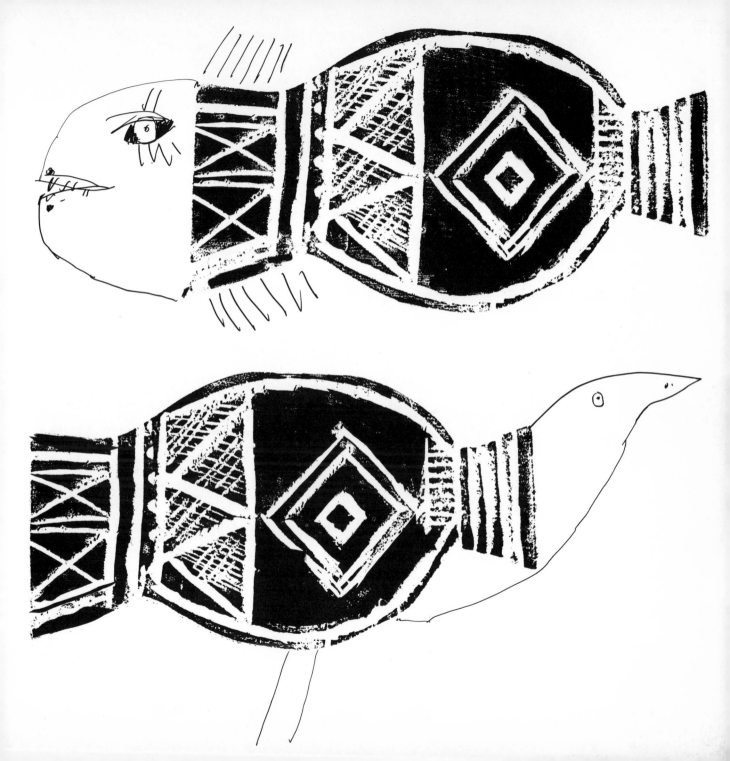

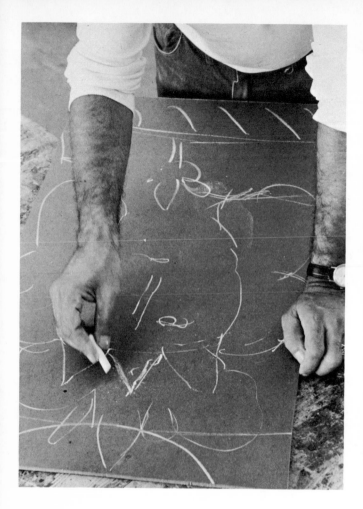

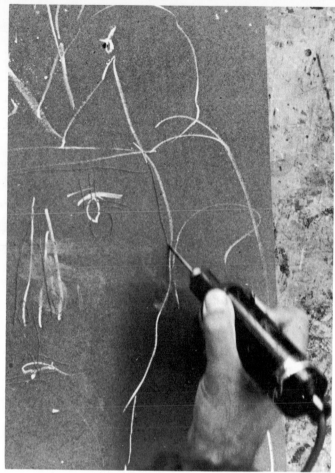

Masonite Project

1. Masonite comes in sheets 4′ x 8′ and in ¼″ and ⅛″ thicknesses. Its surface appears hard, but it is sensitive to any tool including nail scratching and steel brushing. Its size allows for the making of a large woodcut in a very short space of time. To begin with, the design is drawn or sketched into the panel with chalk. The chalk does not permanently mark the surface in any way.

2. Features of the composition are incised into the Masonite surface with a rotary tool and a selection of bits. A nail is used to scratch in further detail and decorative elements.

3. A band saw is used to cut out the outline of the composition. The sawing is easy and fast and takes liberties with the outline drawing, giving the work a feeling of spontaneity. Used freely, the saw makes a line that is unique to it alone. It has its own character.

4. The composition is sandpapered in order to clean the incisions.

5. Further cleaning is done with a steel brush. The brush can also be used to provide a texture to the surface.

6. Ink is mixed with a brayer on a sheet of glass or metal to assure uniform density.

7. It is applied evenly to the Masonite surface, making sure that all composition incisions and scratches are covered.

8. Paper is placed over the composition and pressed against the ink with a roller. This can also be done by hand by pressing with a cloth.

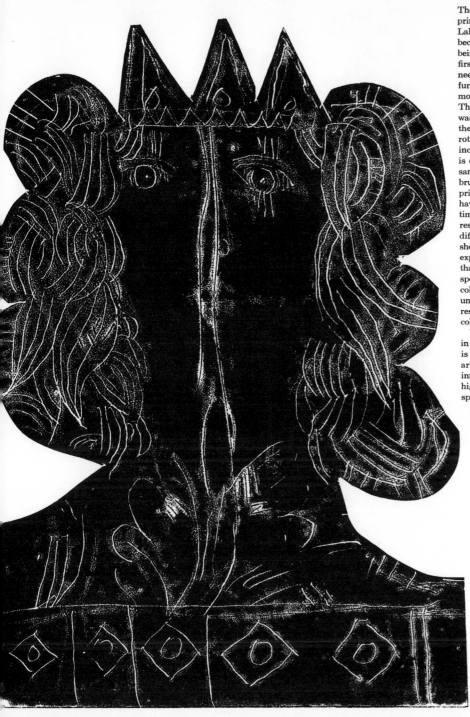

The finished Masonite print by Norman Laliberté. Many times, because the composition being worked is large, the first print will reveal the need for delineating further detail or adding more decorative touches. The Masonite can be washed with kerosene and the surface reworked with rotary bits and nail incisions. The composition is cleaned again with sandpaper and a wire brush, inked, and a new print is pulled. This may have to be done several times before a satisfactory result is achieved. Again, different kinds of paper should be used and experimented with. Stocks that are textured or have special finishes (including color stocks) can provide unique and interesting results, as can different color printing inks.

What should be kept in mind is that the print is but the basic work of art; with a little innovation it can become highly individual and special.

For instance, different color pastels can be applied to the paper over arbitrary areas *before* the paper is applied over the inked woodcut. The printer's ink will seal the pastel into the composition, producing highly interesting effects.

Or, immediately after pulling a print, metallic powder can be sprinkled over the wet composition and then gently shaken off while holding the print in a perpendicular position. The powder clings to the wet areas and an entirely new and surprising composition emerges.

Also, once a print is pulled and dry, it can be cut and reshaped to form the basis of a new work; or it can be enhanced, enlarged or embellished with oil crayons, pastels, color pencils, dyes and inks.

The point is that the woodcut or Masonite print need not be the end in itself; with imagination, it can form the basis of a new and unusual multi-media piece of art.

101

103

108

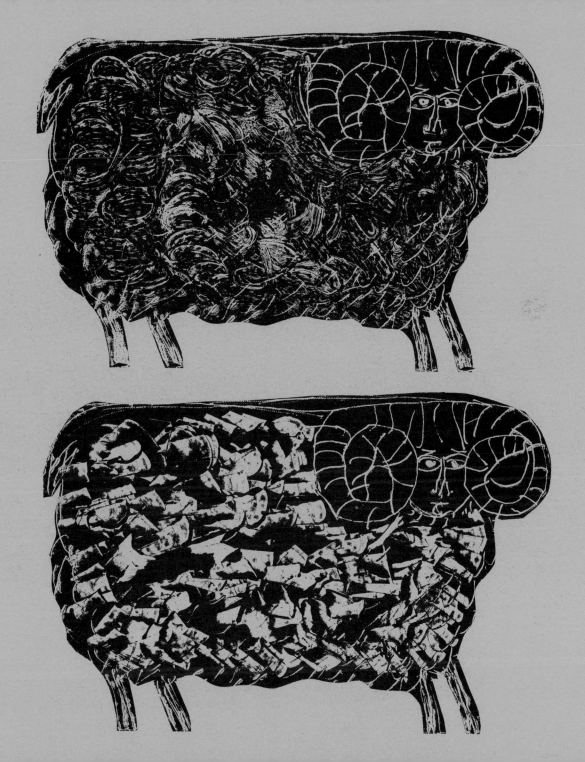